Eric's Talking
Ears

Susan Gates

Illustrated by
Martin Remphry

OXFORD
UNIVERSITY PRESS

OXFORD
UNIVERSITY PRESS

Great Clarendon Street, Oxford, OX2 6DP,
United Kingdom

Oxford University Press is a department of the University of Oxford.
It furthers the University's objective of excellence in research, scholarship,
and education by publishing worldwide. Oxford is a registered trade mark of
Oxford University Press in the UK and in certain other countries

Text © Susan Gates 2002

The moral rights of the author have been asserted

First published in this edition 2016

British Library Cataloguing in Publication Data
Data available

978-0-19-837714-6

1 3 5 7 9 10 8 6 4 2

Paper used in the production of this book is a natural, recyclable product
made from wood grown in sustainable forests. The manufacturing process
conforms to the environmental regulations of the country of origin.

Printed in China by Leo Paper Products Ltd.

Acknowledgements
Cover and inside illustrations by Martin Remphry
Inside cover notes written by Sasha Morton

Contents

1 The Little Blue Book   5

2 Jungle   14

3 What's Going On?   27

4 "You Told Us the Truth!"   35

5 Traitor!   41

6 Rabbit Talk   44

About the author   48

Chapter 1
The Little Blue Book

"What about the things in this box, Dad?" asked Eric. "Shall I throw them out?"

Eric was at the zoo, where Dad was a zoo keeper. It was the summer holidays. He was helping Dad clear out some old cupboards.

"What are they?" asked Dad.

"Yuk!" said Eric. "They're animals' ears! Loads of them!"

"That's disgusting!" said Dad. "Get rid of them!"

"Hang on. They're not real ears, Dad," said Eric, looking again.

He pulled out a pair of big, flappy elephant ears. They were made of grey cloth.

"Good, aren't they?"

He tipped the box on to a table. Lots more ears fell out.

"Someone made all these animal ears," said Eric, puzzled. "What for?"

Dad looked puzzled, too. Then he said, "Wait a second. Is there a book with the ears? And a hat?"

Eric picked a tatty blue notebook out of the heap of ears.

"Is this weird thing a hat?" he asked Dad. It looked like a swimming cap. "But why has it got two little horn things on it?"

"To fit the ears on, of course," said Dad.

"Dad! What are you talking about?" asked Eric, impatiently.*

"All that stuff is really old," explained Dad. "It belonged to a zoo keeper who once worked here. He believed in ear language."

"Ear language?"

"Look in the little blue book," said Dad.

Eric opened the book.

Giraffe Talk, it said. *Three twitches with the left ear means: These flies are annoying me.*

Eric turned to the next page.

Hippo Talk. *Two twitches and a waggle of both ears means: Your water hole is dried up!*

"I get it," said Eric, getting excited. "This zoo keeper thought animals talked to each other by moving their ears?"

"That's right," said Dad.

"And he thought he could talk ear language too!" said Eric. "If he put on this cap!"

He picked up the silly cap and fitted elephant ears on to it.

He pulled it on his head. "What are these strings for?" he asked Dad.

"To make the ears move, of course."

Eric pulled a few strings.

"I can't see. Are my ears moving?"

"They sure are," laughed Dad. "Those elephant ears are flapping like mad! But you'll have to look in the little blue book to find out what you've just said."

"Now I can talk to the zoo animals," said Eric, thrilled. "After I've practised a bit."

Dad laughed. "I bet it doesn't work. It's a crazy idea."

"Oh," said Eric, very disappointed. "Shall I just throw them away then?"

"Might as well," shrugged Dad.

But Eric didn't throw anything away. He packed the ears and the cap and the little blue book back into the box. Then he took the box home with him.

Chapter 2

Jungle

For a whole week, Eric spent hours in his bedroom, secretly practising ear language. Then he went with Dad to the zoo.

"It might work," thought Eric. "You never know. It just might."

At the zoo, Dad went off to feed the monkeys.

"Now," murmured Eric, "who shall I talk to first?"

He began wandering round the zoo.
He felt very nervous. Lots of the animals
were big and fierce and wild. Would
they want to talk to a small, puny human?

The giraffes looked haughty. The lions
were scary. The polar bears were asleep. At
last, he stopped outside the elephant pen.

He put on the cap. He fitted on the big, flappy elephant ears.

"What shall I say first?" he thought.

He gave his ears four twists and two waggles. That meant, "I, a human child, have come to see you!"

The elephants took no notice. They carried on chewing leaves.

"Dad's right," thought Eric, sadly. "This ear language is rubbish!"

He gave it one more try.

"Hello!" he signalled, waggling his left ear. Nothing. None of the big elephants waggled "Hello!" back.

Then two baby elephants wandered up to the fence.

They were called Maya and Miko. Maya began waggling her ears. Three flaps, two left ear waggles.

"Does that mean anything?" thought Eric. He hardly dared to hope. He looked it up in his little blue book.

"Yes, it does!" he cried. He was thrilled. "An elephant is actually talking to me!"

"What is outside the big gates?" Maya was asking him.

"Outside?" thought Eric. "Does she mean outside the zoo?"

He frowned. He looked at the little blue book. It was a very hard question to answer. Ear language had no words for cars or crowds or busy roads.

There was a quiet little park just outside the zoo gates. But there was no word for 'park' in ear language, either.

Maya was getting impatient.

"Ah, here's something!" thought Eric. He'd found a word. It wasn't right, but it would have to do.

Flap, flap went his ears. "There is a jungle outside the big gates," Eric told the baby elephants.

Maya waved her trunk in surprise. "The jungle is so close?"

"Yes," answered Eric.

He thought of the little park. It wasn't exactly a jungle. But it did have a few trees. Anyway, Maya was never going to find out. She was a zoo animal. She was never going to go outside.

"I have heard about the jungle," Miko's ears told him.

"I, too," waggled Maya. "The old elephants tell us stories. The jungle is a wonderful place."

"It is freedom," added Miko, with a longing look in his tiny, bright elephant eyes.

"What are they saying?" thought Eric. He couldn't keep up. Their ears were flapping so fast they were just a blur.

Maya and Miko rushed off, still talking ear language. They seemed really excited.

"Maybe it's because they talked to a human for the first time!" thought Eric.

He felt much more confident now.
He swapped ears. He felt like having a
chat with the hyenas.

The hyenas told jokes about visitors.
They laughed at them all the time. "Look
at that silly man. His face is as red as a
baboon's bottom!"

Eric talked with the timid gazelles next. They seemed to worry a lot. Their ears twitched like mad as they told him, "We are afraid of the crocodiles. They might eat us all up!"

He even dared to have a word with the lions. They seemed very keen to invite him inside their cages.

"Come closer, human child!" waggled an old shaggy-haired lion. His eyes glittered greedily. "Come closer, so I may smell you."

"Er, sorry, I haven't got time," Eric told him. "I'm just off to see some pot-bellied pigs."

"Ah, pigs! I adore pigs," the lion replied, licking his lips.

"I'm really glad I didn't throw these ears out," thought Eric, as he rushed around the zoo. "It's brilliant fun!"

He felt as if he'd been talking ear language all his life!

Chapter 3
What's Going On?

Then, soon after, something strange happened at the zoo. Eric could feel it, as soon as he got out of Dad's car. The gazelles were skipping about. The hyenas were running round in mad circles.

"Why are they all so excited?" Eric wondered.

He headed for the elephant pen. He had to ask Maya and Miko about it.

He fixed on his elephant ears.

Two flicks and a waggle meant:
"What's going on?"

But Maya and Miko didn't run up to greet him.

"What's going on?" he signalled again.

Maya and Miko were far away, at the other side of their pen. Their grey ears seemed busy.

They had lots to say. But they were talking to the kangaroos over the fence, not to him. Eric felt rather left out.

"What are they saying?" he wondered.

He watched their ears. He could keep up now, no matter how fast they moved.

"Don't be silly," Maya was telling the kangaroos. "We elephants can't jump."

"No!" waggled Miko. "We will all find our own way out. The kangaroos can jump fences, the hyenas can dig under them. The elephants will use their strength to push the fences down!"

"And then," Miko told them, "we will all meet up outside the gates in the jungle. The jungle the human child told us about."

"We will all be free!" waggled Maya.

As Eric watched, he felt his heart grow cold. He suddenly realized what they were up to.

The animals were planning a mass break-out! And it was all because of him. He hadn't used the right words. He'd told them there was a jungle outside the zoo.

There were motorways out there. The animals would get run over. And where would they find food? There were no keepers to feed them outside the gates.

"I can't believe this is happening!" thought Eric, horrified.

He had to find out more.

He crept along the side of the elephant pen so he could see what Maya and Miko were saying. He felt like a spy.

"We will escape today!" they were telling the kangaroos. "Pass it on!"

Quickly, the message spread all round the zoo. And there was nothing he could do to stop it.

Eric could hear the whoops as the monkeys got it. Then the roar as it reached the lions. Soon, the whole zoo was buzzing with news of the mass break-out.

Suddenly, Maya saw Eric. "Hello, human child!" she flapped. "Did you hear what we said?"

"Yes," admitted Eric. He didn't want to lie to the animals. They thought he was their friend.

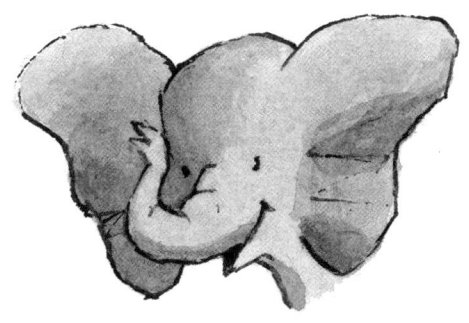

Chapter 4
"You Told Us the Truth!"

"We are very grateful to you!" said Miko. "You told us the truth. The jungle is so close! We cannot wait to get there. It is our dream!"

Eric took hold of the strings that worked his elephant ears. He wanted to waggle, "There is no jungle! You don't understand! It will be terrible out there. You could all die!"

But he just couldn't do it. He couldn't spoil the animals' dreams. He let his hands drop.

"What is that kangaroo asking us?" asked Maya, puzzled. "I can't quite see."

Miko squinted through the fence with his tiny, elephant eyes. "He is asking, 'Does the human child know about our plans? What if he tells the keepers? They will stop our escape!'"

Miko looked angry. His ears flapped furiously. "We can trust the human child! He is on our side!"

Eric felt terrible. There was so much he should say, but he couldn't say any of it.

Eric trudged away from the elephant pen. His mind was in torment. What on earth was he going to do?

Dreadful thoughts were growing like monsters in his brain. He'd only thought about the animals, up to now. He hadn't thought about the danger to humans. What if the lions escaped? With a shudder, Eric thought of the sharp, yellow teeth of the shaggy-haired lion.

"I'm going to have to tell!" Eric decided. "I'm going to *have* to!"

He set off to find Dad. He was still struggling to make up his mind.

He passed the gazelles. They were skipping about in a frenzy. Their ears flickered, "We are going outside to the jungle. The jungle!"

"Oh, no," groaned Eric. "What if they get hit by cars? What if they meet the crocodiles?"

It was no good. He couldn't wriggle out of it any longer. He pushed open the door to the keepers' room. He knew Dad would be having his tea break.

"Dad," he said, in a small shaky voice. "I've got something really important to tell you."

Chapter 5
Traitor!

At first, Dad didn't believe him.

He kept saying, "This is a joke, isn't it?"

Eric insisted, "No, no, honest, Dad, it isn't!"

But a keeper dashed in, shouting, "You'll never believe what's happening! Two gazelles and a kangaroo have just jumped over the fence!"

Then Dad began to believe it.

"Call out all the keepers!" he cried. "This is an emergency!"

The animals' escape was over before
it began. The keepers saw to that. The
two gazelles and the kangaroo were
put back in their pens.

As the kangaroo was led back, he saw
Eric standing with the keepers. His ears
started waggling. Only Eric knew what he
was saying: "We were fools to trust you,
human child!"

The first gazelle twitched her ears angrily. "Traitor!"

The second one told him, "None of us will ever talk to you again!"

On the way home, Eric told himself, "You did it to save the animals. You did it so humans wouldn't get hurt. You *had* to tell!"

The keepers thought he was a hero. But that didn't make him feel any better. The animals thought he was a big sneak. Eric felt really upset about that.

Chapter 6
Rabbit Talk

At home, Eric stood by the dustbin.

"I'm going to throw this ear language stuff away," he decided. It was useless. None of the animals would ever speak to him again. Anyway, it had caused nothing but trouble.

He threw the elephant ears into the bin. Then the gazelle ears. Then all the other ears. At last, there was just one pair of ears at the bottom of his box.

"What are these?" he thought, lifting them out.

They were long and floppy.
They were white and silky.

"Wait a minute, I know!" said Eric.

He'd meant to throw everything away.
But, instead, he ran down to the end of the garden.

Fluffy, his pet rabbit, was out in her run.

Eric searched through the little blue book. He found the page headed *Rabbit Talk*.

He just couldn't stop himself. He fitted the ears on to the hat. He put the hat on his head. Three waggles and two flicks meant, "What is your favourite food?"

"Dandelions," Fluffy told him, blinking her pink eyes.

"And what do you like doing best?" waggled Eric.

"Sunbathing," answered Fluffy.

"At least I've still got one animal to talk to!" thought Eric, happily.

Talking to your pet rabbit wasn't as exciting as talking to lions and elephants.

"But I've had enough excitement for one day," thought Eric.

About the author

I seem to have learned a lot about ears
lately. The other day, my husband, Phil,
told me his mum could waggle her ears
not just both at once, but one at a time.
Then I read about a scientist who made
a cap with animal ears fixed to it, so he
could "talk" to animals. With all these
fascinating facts about ears buzzing
around in my brain, I just had to write a
story like *Eric's Talking Ears*.